Get Published
in Literary
Magazines

Allison K Williams

CORIANDER PRESS

GET PUBLISHED IN LITERARY MAGAZINES

© 2016 Allison K Williams

Coriander Press
1305 W Maple St
Kalamazoo MI 49008
www.idowords.net

Special discounts are available on quantity purchases by corporations, associations, and others. For details, contact the publisher at the address above. Portions of this work originally appeared in the *Brevity* blog.

Printed in the United States of America

Williams, Allison K

Get Published in Literary Magazines / Allison K Williams.

1. Writing—How-to—Manuals. 2. Literary Magazines.
3. Careers in Publishing

ISBN: 978-1-945736-00-1

Second Edition

10 9 8 7 6 5 4 3 2

CORIANDER PRESS

Kalamazoo ✦ Saint Petersburg ✦ Dubai

GET PUBLISHED IN
LITERARY MAGAZINES

ACKNOWLEDGMENTS

With grateful thanks
for the assistance and input of
Dinty W. Moore, Jocelyn Bartkevicius,
Alpha Pomells, Kathryn Rose and
Jay R. Ashworth

Contents

INTRODUCTION

Hi! I'm Allison, and you are an awesome writer who's going to get published. No, really—no matter what your level is or how talented you are, someone, somewhere, wants your work.

Perhaps you're an experienced writer, but you'd like to be published more, or you're having a hard time getting into your dream markets. What's not working in your submission process, and how can you fix it?

Perhaps you're a total beginner, getting ready to send out your first finished and revised work. Where do you start? How do you even know which journals to submit to?

Maybe you're going to write new work to send out. Maybe you already have polished stories, essays or poetry that are ready to find a home. Maybe you'll get ideas for more things to write during this process.

Getting published isn't a lottery or a slim chance—it's

the result of a submission process. In five steps, you'll increase your publish-ability and start your own submission process.

- *ℓ* Identify your goals—what do you want out of publishing your work?

- *ℓ* Learn to evaluate your own level. How good is your work, and what markets should you explore?

- *ℓ* Find literary (and some commercial!) magazines that are appropriate for your genre, topics, and skill level.

- *ℓ* Draft a sleek and simple cover letter that will engage editors with your work, and learn professional format for your writing.

- *ℓ* Send out your first ten submissions.

This symbol indicates an exercise: a specific step you can take to move forward in the submission process.

You'll learn to make an easy spreadsheet to track your work, how to get ideas for new pieces to write, and a simple process for figuring out how and what to submit to where for maximum publishing success.

Along the way, we'll take a look at dealing with rejection, working to improve your level, and what editors think when they look at the submission pile. By the time you've finished the steps in this book, you should have a submission process that you feel confident about, a plan for dealing with rejections, and maybe even a couple of acceptance letters.

Ready?

1. Getting Started vs. Self-Doubt

Are you talented? Does it matter?

Your actual level of talent is only fifty percent of the publishing equation. The other half is persistence, willingness to learn from experience and bravery in equal measure. Many writers struggle with feeling fraudulent—like they aren't entitled to be "a writer," or as if they're waiting for a fairy godmother to show up in a cloud of sparkles, wave her wand and announce, "Now, you may publish!" For some of us, our favorite (or most-feared) professor looms in the back of our head, and we're awaiting symbolic permission from our mentor to move forward.

You're not alone. Most writers spend significant time worrying about whether their work is good or not, whether they can find a home for their poems, essays or stories, whether they should just write for fun, or for a small niche, or let it go entirely. In any artistic field, it's normal to struggle with conflicting emotions:

> 1) I AM SO AWESOME AND AMAZING
>   MY WORK IS THE SHIT AND ONLY
>   PHILISTINES FAIL TO APPRECIATE IT!

and

> 2) Boy. That sucked. Maybe I'll never make
>   anything good again. Maybe I never actually made anything good to start with, and all
>   those people who said they liked it were just
>   lying to make me feel better.

(the above should be read as if it is in a very small, grey font)

On the inside of our heads, those are very special feelings that isolate us from the world and make us completely unique and different from anyone else who has ever made art. In fact, every artist struggles with those feelings, and they are almost boring in their sameness to all the people who are not currently us experiencing them right now.

How can we deal with the tug-of-war between "I'M GREAT!" and "i suck" that can be paralyzing in terms of moving forward with our work?

First, remember you're not alone. Unless we are ignoring everyone else around us while we whine about our own lives, we should be catching on that we're not the only person having these feelings. In fact, we're not even the only person having these feelings right now. If you're in a coffee shop right now, or a library, or a classroom, look left and right—at least two of the people in your field of vision are having a paralyzing moment of self-doubt. We can embrace the validity and commonality of our artist feelings. We can recognize that self-doubt goes hand in hand with artistic achievement, and in fact, self-doubt is necessary in order for us to be ready to learn new things about our own work and how we do it. If we already thought our work was perfect, it would be difficult to learn.

If you're not experiencing self-doubt, congratulations! Enjoy the feeling, and try to remember it later. If you never experience self-doubt, if everything you create is just wonderful, you may not be as good as you think you are. Get a second opinion.

Where we can feel most powerless as artists is in the range of choice available to us. Because every writer's career path is different, we can't point to a corner office and a key to the executive washroom and say, "Great! I made it!" It can be frightening how responsible we must be for our own feelings and our own process. It can be terrifying to realize that no-one else is going to tell us how to begin—we must be brave, we must be persistent, we must give ourselves permission to do the work we want to do, and validate ourselves for significant achievements.

One of the slayers of self-doubt is planning. In the next chapter, you'll start thinking seriously about what you want from your work, and set some specific goals. Sadly, there is no teacher any more to hand out grades and shiny stickers. We have to decide for ourselves: What am I doing here? How will I know when I get it right?

> I want to write a piece that receives comments from people who feel like their own situation has been illuminated. My satisfaction will be the comments themselves.

> I want to self-publish a book. I'll know I did it because I'll hold it in my hand.

> I want to send out five query letters each month. Rejections are the proof I did my job.

> I want to write four non-fiction essays this year. I want to be happy with one, have two worth revising, and one that was practice and goes in a drawer.

> I want to improve my characterization. I'll know I've done this because when I read work by other writers who I admire, I'll recognize similar techniques to those I'm using.

Wallowing in self-doubt is allowed. It's OK to feel shitty about our craft, our work or our publication record. But we have to recognize that the freedom to wallow (there's no Writer Boss to say, "break's over!") also means the freedom to pull up our big-girl pants and move forward with what we've decided we want to do, when we want to do it.

Let's go.

2. What Do You Want?

When I first started submitting work to magazines, I just wanted to have something—anything—that showed my mom I hadn't wasted my time in college.

Later, I was teaching college myself and I needed publication credits for my resume.

Now? I want to get paid.

What do you want to achieve by sending out your work? For the big picture, think about the Three P's:

Publication.

It's rewarding to see your work in print. You want recognition and the satisfaction of sharing your work with readers. It may not matter if the magazine is online-only or hard copy. You want copies on your shelf, or links you can post to social media.

Payment.

You want to make money from writing. You're more likely to pick a venue based on a per-word or per-piece rate. You may focus more on commercial/mass-market magazines and websites rather than strictly literary journals.[1]

Prestige.

You want your work to appear in places whose names will look good on your resume, either to propel you towards more publication, or to build an academic career that requires publication. You value being "taken seriously" as a writer.

Are you an emerging writer who wants to break into literary magazines? Do you want to find out if getting published is even possible? Your goal may be Publication. You'll want to focus on finding the best fit by matching your level to the magazine's level without shooting too high at first, then raising your level as you gain publication credits.

Maybe you already have some publications in smaller magazines or local indie journals, but you'd like to have bigger names on your resume. It would be

1. We won't cover the "pitch" process in this book, but when submitting already-written work, the process is the same. If your focus is mass-market, the MediaBistro website is a good place to start finding out more.

a dream come true to open your favorite literary journal and see your work, maybe even in the same issue as a writer who's influenced you. Seek out Prestige. Start by thinking about magazines you've heard great things about, or that you admire and love to read.

If you've had some publication successes already, maybe you'd like writing to be your part-time or even full-time job. Pay close attention to which magazines pay in cash, and send your submissions to those markets first. You want Payment, but it's important to balance cash flow with increasing prominence, so your acceptances gradually become more important and profitable.

Freewrite or think about what you want. What does success look like to you? Is your mom proudly showing copies of a magazine to her friends? Do you have a small, steady income from writing? Are you building credits for a teaching resume or future grant/residency applications?

Thinking about your ultimate, big-picture goal helps you choose where to submit. For example, I want to make money from writing, teaching and public speaking. I need a mix of cash and resume-building credits. When I'm considering where to send a piece, or looking for ideas to write something new aimed at a particular publication, I look at three things:

1) Do they pay? 'No' isn't a deal-breaker every time, but I want to know up front.

2) Are they prestigious? Sometimes that makes up for low or no pay. See Chapter Four for how to figure out a magazine's fame.

3) Do I like what I read in them? Is the level of writing about where I am? It's silly to submit to a journal I don't enjoy or think isn't good quality, and a waste of time to send my work to a place publishing only Pulitzer-Prize winners and MacArthur geniuses.

When you know your big picture goals, get specific:

Do you want to write for magazines? Internet sites? Literary or commercial? Newspapers? (Op-ed, fashion, lifestyle?) A regular column? Your own blog? Fiction or nonfiction? Poetry or prose? Personal essay or journalism?

Do you want to write books? Fiction? What genre? Non-fiction? For what audience? What short pieces could you place to build your personal level of recognition and authority ("platform")?

What's your timeline for results? How long are you willing to put in your best effort before changing focus?

What's your big dream? Think about the small steps you can take towards your big dream. For example, I'd like to be in the New Yorker and on This American Life. That's not going to happen yet. But I can try every day for a publication credit that brings me closer to playing in that ballpark. I pitch radio stories and make my own podcasts. I do some work for free—such as blogging on literary magazine sites—that I believe gets me closer to the big dream.

Working for Free

Throughout this book you'll hear me harp on about money money money. It's one of my primary considerations as a writer, and as a professional artist I want to be paid for my work. That said, it can be a very good choice to trade payment for prestige, even if you are otherwise focused on selling your work.

One of the credits I'm most pleased with is the *New York Times*, and I've been in there several times. The first time, though, was a blog entry responding to a call for stories about spending the holidays abroad, and it was published without payment.

What made it worthwhile?

- I already had the essay written. It was easy to polish it for an hour and hit send.

- It's a big name publication. Exposure might actually mean something in a media outlet of that size (most of the time, "good exposure" just means "work for free"). It looks good on my resume.

- It's a publication I admire, respect and read. I felt honored to be included. It felt like a foot in the door.

- It was when I had few publications on my resume and needed the credit.

Similarly, I have several writer friends who blog for the *Huffington Post*, a notorious non-payer. Those writers find it worthwhile to write regularly for an audience larger than they could command on their own. It's a chance to build a body of work that they can later use as clips when they approach other media outlets. And I've submitted to some big name literary magazines without knowing or caring if they pay—I'd just like to be among their excellent authors.

When you have an opportunity that's not in line with your primary goal (payment, prestige, publication), weigh it carefully—it might still be a good deal.

3. How Good Are You?

Before I was a full-time writer, I was a professional circus performer, an aerialist and fire-eater (really!). I grew up attending the circus and as a kid, was blown away by the acts I saw. Now, going to the circus is a much different experience. When I see trapeze artists and fire-eaters, I don't just say "wow!"—I start thinking about what makes it wow.

Check out those transitions.

Love that she did that move as a one-arm instead of two.

Way to raise the difficulty level on that move!

Cheap trick, but the audience loves that one.

I'd never have thought to go from there to there with that transition.

Her moves are really simple, but she's so graceful.

Not a lot of skill, but I love her attitude—she can really sell it.

And if I saw something great, I'd try to copy it with a new spin that made it my own.

Improving as a writer works the same way. We go through three steps:

- Being impressed

- Recognizing tools and elements

- Being able to use the tools and elements consciously in our own work.

1) Wow!

We read something, we like it, we read more in that genre or by that author. We develop a taste for a particular style or writer. We look forward to the next thing they publish. We get to know their body of work and love being surprised by a new structure or character. We take pleasure in discovering a new author, or being part of the social media conversation around a particular book.

2) Identifying the tools used in impressive writing

Once we've enjoyed being impressed, it's time to think analytically. How did the author impress us?

What tools did she use? What about the book thrilled or moved us?

Check out those transitions.

Love that she told that whole story in just 700 words.

The way that structure looped around was so unexpected and satisfying.

OK, it's trash, but it's good trash.

I'd never have thought to put those two parts of the story next to each other, but it makes them both better.

It's so well-told – not a wasted word.

Great voice.

3) Using those tools ourselves

Once we can regularly identify writing tools and techniques, the final step is employing those techniques in your own work. After you've spent time consciously self-editing, even first drafts will begin to incorporate more skilled writing as your tools become habits.

Wait—I don't need this whole paragraph, the transition is implied.

Too many adverbs, I'm going to punch up the dialogue instead.

What if I told this with a different timeline instead of just chronologically?

I'm having so much fun writing something commercial!

Yes, this is where that description goes, and it shows what the hero is thinking.

OK, I can totally trim this down.

What if I did the next draft in first person?

Going through these three steps is not a one-time thing. Every time your work improves, you'll get better at analyzing others' work, which in turn allows you to get even better. It's a virtuous circle.

How good is your writing right now? And how can you tell? It's hard to judge the quality of our own work. Most of our friends are more supportive than critical—thank goodness.

But in order to figure out where your work belongs, you need to know how good it is. New Yorker and Paris Review good? Community college literary magazine good? Most of us are somewhere in between.

Since it's hard to judge your own work, start by judging someone else's.

Step One

Pick a venue—whether paper journal or Internet site—you want to be in. One you enjoy reading, so you have a sense of their usual material. (It's always a good idea to be familiar with where you want to be published.) In the magazine, read something in your genre—a story, a poem or an essay. Can you tell if it's good or not? If you don't understand it, or you're "not getting it," it's either much worse or much better than you are right now. That's where looking up the magazine's and the author's reputations can help (more on that in Chapter Four). If they've won a Pulitzer Prize, it's probably you.

Step Two

The piece you read—Was it good? Did you find yourself hooked when you read it the first time? Are there sentences you wish you wrote? At the end, do you feel like you've had an emotional experience? If it's not good, it might be an exception. Read another piece. If you hit three in a row you think are bad, either your work is better than this magazine, or your taste is different. Go back to Step One and pick something else.

Step Three

When you get to a good piece, look up the author. Do they have a bunch of other publication credits? In magazines you've heard of? Won any prizes, like a Pushcart or an artists' grant from their state? This starts to tell you the level of the authors already in that magazine. Do you feel like you fit in? If you're a newbie, do any of the authors have "emerging writer" in their bio, or no credits listed?

Step Four

Take another look at the piece. Like you're in an English class. Why is it good? Can you identify specific tools the writer used, like structure, concept, voice, or characterization? Being able to see those tools at work can be a sign your work is getting closer to what you're reading.

Step Five

Think about something you've written recently. Do you use those same (or similar) tools in your writing, on purpose? When people read your piece, do they get a feeling that's as strong as the one you got about the piece you just read? Strong enough to tell you about it? If you can answer "yes" to these questions, you may be a good fit for this venue.

Step Six

The tough one—think about the way your work is received right now. Does anyone ask to read it? Not just when you ask for feedback, or when it's your turn in the writing group. Do people not related to you read your work and approach you to ask for more, or tell you they liked it? That's a good sign you're at a publishable level. If you've been timid, or haven't had a chance yet to get your work into a public forum, blogging, or writing-community sites like Wattpad and Sixfold, can help you reach readers you don't know personally.

Other key questions to determine whether your work is at a publishable level:

- If you've been in a contest, where did you place or rank? Did you gain any new readers? Did people start following your blog because they liked your work?

- If you have started submitting, are you getting all polite form rejections, or have any come as personal letters with specific feedback on your piece? Have you gotten any "please send something else another time" emails? (They mean it!) Anything that says "this was almost there for us"?

- If you're in a writers' group, or you've taken a class or workshop, have you have you ever read your piece aloud, then had a moment of silence before someone said, "Wow"?

- When your writing group or chosen reader responds to your work, do you get more "picky" feedback about phrases, sentences or details, rather than global feedback on structure, story, or writing habits that are present throughout the piece? This is one place where respectful, direct, and extensive criticism reflects a higher quality of work than enthusiastic-but-generic encouragement.

- Do other writers whose work you admire have positive and specific feedback about yours? Do they suggest places you might submit your work? Has a workshop teacher suggested you start submitting?

- Can you identify a story or book's structure, voice, craft, concept and plot? Do you consciously use those elements in your own work? When you read something that isn't working, can you tell what needs more work? Do you have specific ideas for how to fix it? Can you tell when your own work is not your best, or part of a piece is weaker than the rest?

- Can you write a first draft, or polish something that's due, even when you don't feel inspired and don't want to write? Do you have some specific techniques for writing when you don't feel like it but you know you "should," or have a deadline to meet?

- Can you look at your older work and point to specific things you've gotten better at?

One last step—ask someone you respect as a writer to give it to you straight. If you phrase it as "what magazines do you think this piece might be right for?" you're more likely to get a useful answer as well as a supportive one.

How to raise your level

Our level grows as writers when we can appreciate a piece that's good, identify the tools that made it good, and use those tools in our own work.

Read a lot—but read systematically. Read scholarly work, reviews and criticism as well as the actual pieces. Read groups of stories or poems together, exploring a genre or a structure or a theme. If you like a book, find out if the author wrote anything shorter that was published in a journal, and read that. Read with a critical eye, as well as reading for fun.

Read your fellow early-career writers, or other unpublished writers. It's a lot easier to identify issues in someone else's work, and then you're more likely to recognize them in your own. This will sound mean—and it's not the last mean thing I'm going to say—but it's comforting to read very bad work and say to yourself, "Whew! I know I'm better than that!"

Build critique relationships with people who will praise you and people who will cut you to the quick. It's worth investing the time over months or years when you've found someone you really click with. I have two longtime critique partners with whom I exchange work and give feedback. Friend Horror Writer started confident—we were already friends, he knew he was good and he knew he had help to offer me. Friend Essayist was a beginner and we didn't have a close relationship at first (we do now!). Over the course of two years we went from gently suggesting and questioning each other's work—I didn't want to hurt her feelings, she perceived my level as higher than hers and didn't yet know how great her instincts were—to a point where we each felt we could say "that's not working: fix it!" to the other one an hour before deadline.

Write when you're not inspired, when you don't feel like it. See what your base level of craft is when you're not cruising on an adrenaline high. Not all your work will be good, but it can all be grammatically correct (unless deliberately not) and employing purposeful writing techniques.

Becoming a better writer is like teaching yourself a class. And you can take a class, too—at the junior college, with the writing group at the local bookstore or through Meetup, or by ordering some texts that teach writing and doing the exercises at home in your room. If you're too broke to order books, there are a ton of free writing exercises online—everything from specific websites teaching writing to syllabi and assignments for college classes.

4. What's Your Market?

I know a writer who was really, really irate she didn't win a contest held by one of the most prestigious literary magazines in the USA. She was an emerging writer with no publication credits and no critique partners (critique wasn't well-received). When she didn't win or place, she wrote a long blog post about privilege.

Privilege had little to do with it. Yes, privilege does affect publication, especially for people of color and people from working-class or financially disadvantaged backgrounds[2], but this was not her issue. The issue was that she wasn't yet ready to compete on that playing field.

2. This is a huge issue that I don't cover in this book. If you want to find out more, you might start with recent essays on writing and privilege by Roxanne Gay at *The Rumpus*, Lorraine Berry at *Literary Hub*, and Andrea Bennett at *Hazlitt*. Links to those essays are in the Resources chapter.

It's like being the best swimmer in your neighborhood pool and getting mad that you didn't medal in the Olympics. It's not that you can't win a contest or get a grant or be published in a big-name venue without a string of previous credits and an MFA—in fact, the number-two complaint from MFAs is "We didn't learn anything about how to get published." (Number one is "There are no jobs for Creative Writing MFAs".) It's that you have to find your level. Why be frustrated with endless rejections from the "top ten" when you could have a fantastic editorial experience with #47, improve your work and gain a credit that helps you raise your level?

What's out there?

Let's start with a field trip. Head out to your local bookstore—bonus points for indies, and they often have more literary magazines. Check out what's on the shelves—what magazines make you want to open them up? Buy some and read them! (If you're broke this week, head down to the library; you already paid for that.)

The places best for your work are probably the ones you love to read. What do you subscribe to, in your inbox or your mailbox? What literary or culture websites do you check every day? Chances are good you've already got an idea of their style. Start thinking about what pieces you have that fit that tone.

What do you love to write? If you're a romance writer

or a mystery writer, there are magazines for those genres. If you're a poet, you're spoiled for choice—most literary magazines have poetry, and some publish only poetry.

If nonfiction's your bag, some magazines focus on creative nonfiction and personal essays, and a lot of commercial markets also publish essays. What's in your local newspaper, especially the Sunday Style or Life or Books section? Next time you're waiting in the express checkout behind the lady who totally has thirteen items when the sign clearly says ten, leaf through some magazines and see who publishes personal stories, fiction, poetry, and essays. A lot of major magazines—*Glamour, Marie Claire, Real Simple*—have a dedicated space for literary work.

It's useful to get a couple of subscriptions to magazines you like—and a lot of places that charge a submission fee give you a subscription or the most recent issue. Many contests also include a subscription for the price of entry. Start building your literary library. Yes, literary magazines are expensive—most don't have substantial advertising revenue. Ask the public library what they do with out-of-date magazines—you may be able to pick up some past issues. Some go up for sale cheap on Amazon or eBay (*McSweeney's*, in particular, has beautiful, heavy, hardbound issues that are correspondingly pricy, but can be found on eBay.) And lots of magazines put all or part of their content online for free.

Finally, start keeping track of your favorite authors. Read their website bios—where have they had work published? Are any titles starting to pop up again and again?

Choosing

All right. You're a hard-working, level-improving writer with a pile of magazines you like—and you've ruled out some you hate. Now it's like dating. Are they good enough for you? Are you good enough for them? Let's start stalking our favorites.

As you narrow down your possible markets, remember that you want to send your work to a place you love to read, and that's right for your level of work. You figured out how good you are back in Chapter Three, now let's start judging the magazines...

["The Dating Game" theme plays]

Behind door number one: He's a multiple Pushcart Prize-winner, featuring the work of Stuart Dybek and Dinty W. Moore. Based at a prominent university with a strong creative writing department, he comes out four times a year and maintains a stylish website. And writers, he pays contributors $25/page, up to $200.

Behind door number two: She's a small-press indie journal published in your home town!

Founded by a recent MFA graduate and her friends, you'll notice some overlap between the names on the masthead and the writers in the pages. But that poem on page fifteen is a real stunner, and this month's cover is striking. She doesn't know how much longer she'll be in business, but while she lasts, contributors get two copies of the issue they're printed in.

And, behind door number three: This commercial magazine aims for women who want a balanced life. There's a personal essay every month on the back page, and a short story somewhere in the middle. On pages 27 and 68, surprise! It's poetry! Are you a woman, or someone who writes for a female reader? At a dollar-fifty a word, this little beauty might be the perfect match for you.

OK—let's get serious. The easiest way to tell the level of a magazine is to check out what other people are saying about them. You can use online ranking lists (some are listed in Resources) to identify "big deal," "mid-career," and "entry-level" magazines. From there, start looking for signals that the publication is strong. If any of the authors in their pages has been a Poet Laureate of their state or of the nation—I'm looking at you, Maya Angelou—or if they've won a Pulitzer Prize, a Nobel Prize, or a National Book Award, it's probably a pretty good magazine. You may want to win some similar prizes, or be recognized with a grant, a fellowship, or an award before you send off to that big boy.

Keep checking out those magazine websites, and you'll also start seeing some of the same authors mentioned as past contributors. That helps you group magazines by quality and reputation. And it helps you scale your expectations. If they've got Amy Hempl, Stuart Dybek, Sherman Alexie and George Saunders on their list, they're a reasonably big deal, they're getting a lot of submissions and you'll be competing with a lot more authors for page space.

The Pushcart Prizes are given every year to the best fiction, poetry and essays published by small presses and in literary magazines. If a magazine has won a bunch of Pushcarts, or the authors mention Pushcarts in their bios, that's a sign of quality and reputation.

Start making a list of places you'd like to send work.

Think about what you like to read. What magazines are exciting to buy? What newspaper column do you turn to first? What website is top of your bookmarks? You're more likely to be publishable when you're familiar with what they already write, and you like it.

Use online sources to find magazines specific to your genre or topics. *The Review Review*'s lists are great, including "Magazines that Pay," "Audio Literary Magazines," and "Magazines about Food." Look on Duotrope and New Pages (again, see Resources). Google "Pushcart Prize" and look at the most recent lists of winners. Start getting a sense of the big players, the medium players, and the home teams. Rankings change from year to year, but you'll start to see the same names show up on multiple lists.

Sample some online literary magazines. Set a goal—maybe you dip into one new magazine a week, or five every month. Some of them have downloadable PDFs (like *Five Dials* and *The Missing Slate*), so if you're a hardcore reader-of-paper, you can print them out.

Leaf through literary magazines at your local bookstore or library. Which ones would you be delighted to see your name in? What journals are regional or from your state? A geographic connection can sometimes be a door in, and most local publications are less competitive. Do note that many journals with a state in the title (*Missouri Review, Florida Review*) are not specifically seeking work from or about that region. Naming a journal after the state or university of origin is a long tradition, not a call for themed submissions.

Look up the authors you like to read—where have they been published? Many literary novelists have had stories in magazines, too. What was their career path? Did they get an MFA or are they self-taught? What age did they start writing at? What awards have they won? How long did it take them to get published when they started? What background do they have relative to their work?

As you browse, make sure to notice prestige and/or payment if these are your priorities. Magazines with advertising in them are more likely to pay. Literary journals often specify payment (or lack thereof) on the submissions page on their website.

What about contests?

Some contests are terrific. Some are scams. Until you learn to notice the telltale signs, enter only contests that have been around for a while, rather than first efforts. Check Preditors and Editors (http://pred-ed.com) and Writer Beware! (http://accrispin.blogspot.com) for warnings about contests and publishers who are scams or not going to benefit you in proportion to the cost of entry. Generally, if they have a list of badges, trophies, stickers and anthologies you can purchase to announce your win, it's a money-making venture, not a literary contest.

Look for contests that have more than one prize, not just a single winner. This can be good—more chances to win. This can also be bad—if your work is third place, and they publish all the winners but only pay the first place author, you just gave your story away for free. Most places don't publish reprints, and that includes contest winners. Make sure the prestige is worth it, and keep an eye out for contests with cash prizes for second and third place, too. If you're seeking Prestige, it's valuable to be in a top-tier journal and have their prize on your resume, even honorable mention. Or maybe the judge is a writer you admire and would love to have read your work.

Remember that a literary contest is not a lottery. Assess your chances. Read the past winners' work—are you in that league? Read any follow-up interviews with last year's winning authors. Read judges' reports about their ranking process and what they looked for. For example, The Bridport Prize (https://www.bridportprize.org.uk/) has years of judges' reports, worth reading even if you don't enter that contest.

You can also focus on contests where you get something for your fee, maybe a copy of the magazine with the winning entries or a year's subscription. Some contests include feedback, either from judges or from other entrants, and that can be very worthwhile.[3] Be aware that in contests with prestigious judges, your work may still navigate one or more levels of pre-readers, who may be the editorial staff or graduate students. It's not uncommon that the big-name judge only sees ten or fifteen entries.

I recommend not entering a contest where the entry fee is more than 5-10% of the prize, unless you have a strong piece, it's a great judge, and you're very confident you'll be in the top tier of entrants. If there's a $20 entry fee, there had better be a $1000 prize, or a subscription you're looking forward to reading.

---

3. One contest with feedback and a low entry fee is Sixfold, and my experience was that I got useful feedback from my fellow contestants. www.sixfold.org.

Some well-respected contests are those from the *Missouri Review*, *Bellingham Review*, *Iowa Review* and *Crab Orchard Review*. Magazines with Pushcart Prizes (more on that later) are usually holding legit contests.

If you're a strong writer, and you know your work is already on a par with what the journal publishes, contest winnings can be a source of income. Several of the top contests have prizes of $2000 or $5000; In the UK, the Bridport Prize gives a number of cash awards, topping out at five thousand pounds—and they accept entries from writers all over the world.

What about writing for a specific magazine?

You probably already know the first step: read everything you can in the specific venue in which you want to publish. As Sara Mosle wrote in the *New York Times*,

> *Malcolm Gladwell, author of The Tipping Point and a New Yorker staff writer, told me how he prepared, years ago, to write his first "Talk of the Town" story. "Talk" articles have a distinct style, and he wanted to make sure he got the voice straight in his head before he began writing. His approach was simple. He sat down and read 100 "Talk" pieces, one after the other.*

I've done the same with the *New York Times*' Modern Love column, even sitting down and analyzing story structure like I did back in high school English class, and I'm sure I'm not the only one. I have pages in my notebook with lists of potential stories, organized by what venues I think might buy them. When it's time to write, I flip through and choose an idea to work on.

The Detective Process

I read an essay at *Green Mountains Review* and liked it very much. I flipped to the author's bio:

AARON GILBREATH has written essays for the *New York Times, Paris Review, Kenyon Review, The Believer, Brick,* and the *Threepenny Review,* and articles for *Oxford American, Virginia Quarterly Review* and *Flavorwire.* His book *This Is: Essays on Jazz* comes out in fall, and Future Tense Books published his chapbook *A Secondary Landscape* in 2013. He's working on a book about crowding and lives here [link to his website].

I've never heard of this guy before, but I like his work, and his bio includes journals and magazines I know to be high-level and widely read. He's probably been in a lot more magazines than he lists, which means he's listing the biggest/most important credits he's got—so I tick them in my sheet.

5. Get Systematic

When seeking publication, you'll need to track two key things:

1) Where you want to submit

2) Where you did submit, what you sent them, and when

As you look up magazines, note down the information that's right for you. Remind yourself of your goals from Chapter Two. Do they pay? Are they prestigious? Are they at a level where your work is likely to get published?

A spreadsheet is usually more useful than a list in a document, and you can make one in Excel or on Google Docs or whatever program makes you happy. You can also use a Word doc, or Pages, or a legal pad beside your desk. But you Must. Keep. Track. (I'll tell you why in just a minute.)

Customize your spreadsheet so that it reflects your goals.

If you're looking for prestige, note down which magazines have won prizes, or had pieces included in anthologies like *Best American Short Stories*. Check them out on The Review Review and see what other writers say about them. When you see that an author you admire has been published in a particular magazine, note that down.

If publication is your primary goal, focus on places that are at or slightly below your level. Look for whether they welcome "emerging writers"—a lot of magazines say that right on their website. Or look for very specialized magazines that suit your niche—poetry about food! nonfiction under 300 words!—and are likely to get fewer submissions for you to compete with.

Keep records on every publication you look up. Who's right for you? Who's not worth the bother? After you've checked out a hundred magazines, some of them blur together. Writing down the "NOs" will save you from researching the same magazine twice.

> *Auuggghhhhh…paperwork! I didn't become a writer to deal with pay—perrr—worrrrk!*

You can be an artist for fun, or you can be an artist to make money, or to be read, or to be known. The more you want to achieve these things, the more paperwork you'll have to deal with. But even if you're writing for fun (and that's a great reason to write!), you can end up being accidentally rude if you don't keep track of your submissions.

Oh, wow! Cool Kid Review accepted my poem, "Meditations on My Coffee Shop Existence While Smoking An Obscure Brand of Cigarettes." That's great!

Oh wait. I think I sent that poem to a couple other places, because I knew Cool Kid Review might take a while to get back to me. Now…where did I send it? Crap. I have no idea.

Simultaneous submissions are almost always OK (more on this in Chapter Seven). That means sending out a single piece to more than one place at a time. Journals often take a long time to respond, so don't make one venue your only submission. Waiting six months for a rejection eats a lot of time. They aren't being jerks—a lot of them are run by student labor and everything slows down in the summer, at exam time, holidays, etc. And many journals are a labor of

	A	B	C	D	E	F	G	H	I
1	Name	Editor (of you)	Website	Print?	Pay?	Publishes	Response	Process	Notes
2	Genius Literary	Jane Doe	www.genius-mag.com	Yes	$50	Twice yearly	6 months	Submittable	Themed winter issue, has published Author I Love,
3	Cool Kids Review	Shonda Smit	www.ckreview.org	No	no	monthly	2 months	Email	Author I Like, also emerging Recommended by workshop leader
4									
5									
6									
7									

An exmaple submission tracking spreadsheet

love. Sometimes it's one or two busy writers who are also teachers, reading late at night in their Copious Free Time. But for commercial outlets (consumer magazines, culture websites, newspapers) simultaneous submissions are a no-no. They tend to respond to submissions fairly quickly (if you haven't heard back in three weeks, you can usually assume it's a pass), and editors don't want to waste their time reading your piece if you get it accepted somewhere else three days later.

When you get an acceptance, you must notify everyone else they can't have it. If you used Submittable or another online submissions system, it's easy to withdraw online. Otherwise, send a brief, polite email informing them your work has been published elsewhere.

> *Thank you for considering my poem, "Meditations on My Coffee Shop Existence While Smoking An Obscure Brand of Cigarettes." I must withdraw it from your consideration; it's been accepted at* X Magazine. *I look forward to sending you another piece soon.*

Sign your first and last name in case the journal organizes submissions by author name.

There's a certain satisfaction in withdrawing—too slow, bro! Someone else wanted me!—and (while this doesn't happen very often), the magazine you've withdrawn from may look more carefully at your work in the future so they don't lose their chance.

Create a spreadsheet or table of magazines you know about, and ones to research more. An entry can be fully filled in, or just write in the title you hear about, to look up later.

Make a column for what you care about the most—maybe you only write travel essays, or on motherhood, or formal poetry, so you need a magazine that includes or focuses on your topic. Maybe you really want to be in physical print, so you note whether a magazine is online-only. My spreadsheet has a column for whether or not a magazine pays. Every time I read a submission call, or see a magazine mentioned in someone's bio, I check back with my spreadsheet, and add the title or update my notes on that journal. If they don't pay, they aren't for me. Your goals may be different.

Then visit the magazine's website, and read a print copy if you can get one. Does it look professional? Would you be proud to have your work showcased here? Are they prestigious? Are they at a level where your work is likely to get published? Many magazines will say on their websites that they welcome "emerging writers," and that's worth noting down.

Look for the technical things you need to know. What are their submission policies? Are they accepting work right now? Do they only take mailed submissions? Do they have any theme issues coming up? Do they run a regular column or section with a specific focus?

Read a couple of pieces from their archives and see if you're in the right ballpark. Is the selection of work in a style or tone you'd fit in with?

Well damn, that's a lot of reading.

Yes. That's why you should read where you want to be published. If it's not a pleasure to read their magazine, your work may not be a good fit. If you enjoy reading and look forward to each issue or site update, that's a good sign that you are the target reader and thus will know more about what their readers want, and what their editors are likely to publish. Read where you want to publish, publish where you like to read.

When I first started getting serious about writing, I added three magazines a week to my list. This could be looking up a new journal, or filling in details on three where I had the name and website and nothing else. Some days I did more. Right now I have about 500 titles (magazines, websites, newspapers and radio shows) on my list, and full details on about a hundred of them. It's a big job. Break it into tiny-but-regular bites.

Social media can also be useful, especially if you're part of a writer's group that focuses on submission opportunities. I'll often screenshot a call for entries as a fast way to note the details, and I keep a folder on my desktop with those photos.

Another of my categories is "Prestige." Every time I read something good about the magazine, or I see a big-name author mention them in a bio, I put an extra plus in that column. If I read a piece I really like in any journal, I check out that author's credits, and put a tick-mark next to anywhere they've been published. I'll also add magazines from their credits to my list if I don't already have them.

I highlight places that are "send ASAP!" and grey out "don't bother" publications (usually because there is no pay plus no prestige, or they have a high submission fee, or I dislike the work I've read in them).

This gradual process lets me know who's worth submitting to, who's on my level, and who might be a bigger deal than I'm ready for. (If they've got Nobel Laureates in the magazine, I'm not there yet.) There are also the side benefits of becoming familiar with more authors' work, and building my own literary citizenship by participating as a reader.

Well damn, that's a lot of work.

Yes. And if you are not a person who enjoys sitting in climate-controlled comfort, exploring the world's greatest and easiest-to-access information network on your personal piece of expensive and powerful technical equipment, perhaps you should take up coal mining.

Isn't that a little mean?

Yes. Writing is fun. Getting published is work. You don't have to get published, and you don't have to do the work, but you're not going to get very much of the former without a lot of the latter.

But most places only publish people they know.

1) That is incorrect. Connections help, but hard work can often take its place. Besides, once you get a few credits under your belt, you will be one of the people they know.

2) Those people are also working hard, every day, to write good material and send it out. You know how bad it sucks to get a rejection email? It's worse when it comes from your friend.

Submissions can be a confusing and intimidating process. But if you get systematic, you'll be able to take specific, measurable steps to polish and improve your work, figure out who wants it, and keep track of where it goes. You can do it. There is no magic, only practice.

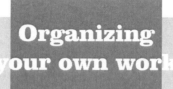

Organizing your own work

Once you get started in the submission process, it can be challenging to remember what you wrote and where it is on the computer. I keep multiple drafts of each story or essay in a single folder, then nest those folders in folders for Fiction, Nonfiction, and Poetry. I also separate the "done" pieces and the works-in-progress in each main category.

```
Fiction
   Story A
      Story A Draft 1 10-17-12
      Story A Draft 2 11-4-13
      Story A Draft 3 1-5-15
Fiction WIP
   Story B
      Story B Draft 1 2012-10-17
      Story B Draft 2 2013-11-04
      Story B Draft 3 2015-01-05
Published
      Essay A
      Story C
      Poem A
      Essay B
```

When you're saving multiple drafts, put a date in the file title. When you're scanning for the most recent version to send out, your computer will show you when you last opened each draft, not when you finished that draft.

6. Cover Letters and Format

Most of your submissions will be in a standard format and accompanied by a cover letter or short biographical statement. The point of the cover letter is to briefly attach the idea that a really terrific person wrote this piece. Note that "terrific" in this case can mean "well-published and famous," or it can mean "emerging and exciting" or it can mean "I, the editor will get to discover someone" or it can mean, "follows directions and sends what we asked for."

Follow directions.

Follow directions.

Follow directions.

Authors who follow directions send the message "I listen and pay attention, and I'm a pleasure to work with." Pleasant, brief cover letters set up that you are a professional (or a professional-to-be, and the editors won't know the difference at this stage). A standard format shows that you are aware of current practices in the writing world and are doing your part as a literary citizen.

There are few authors whose work is so special they don't have to follow directions for submission. If you are one of them, you already know. (If you are correct in your self-assessment, congratulations on your recent prizes and publications—why not pass this book along to someone who needs it more? If you are incorrect, this guide will not help you.)

FORMAT

If you do a web search on "standard format," you'll come up with quite a few variations. Many publications have their own specifications on how they would like your piece formatted. Some may seem capricious at best—I once wrote "NO" next to a magazine on my spreadsheet that detailed font, margins, spacing, spelling, ink color, biographical statement length, size of author photo, and several different permissions statements. On the other hand, that magazine has probably had enough experience plowing through poorly formatted submissions to try to save themselves some headaches.

If there are specific directions for the journal you've chosen, follow them. If not, do your best to make your writing clean and visually inviting:

- Reasonable amounts of white space

- Double-spaced lines (except poetry)

- Your name and contact information on the top of the first page

- Start the first page about a third of the way down

- When in doubt, 12-point Times New Roman or another serif font, 1-inch margins.

- Numbered pages (page X of Y is often useful to someone who prints out submissions to read at home and the dog jumps on them and they drop every-thing. Not that I know anyone that's ever happened to.)

Do not:

- Write "copyright" or the copyright symbol on your submission. All writing is under copyright protection from the moment it's recorded in a fixed form. And no-one is out to steal your work. Really, truly. Anyone with enough visibility to make any money off stealing writing is someone who already has their own work. It's mildly insulting to the publication that you seem to be suggesting they might plagiarize you, and it's the mark of an amateur.

- Send a photo unless specifically requested.

- Use a font that expresses your individuality or the theme of your piece. Be creative in the writing, be standard in the font. Editors often wear reading glasses—be kind. Don't use fun fonts, colors other than black, more than one font, pictures, or huge swaths of bold or italics.

- *ᶠ* Use a background color. See previous point.
- *ᶠ* Try to circumvent length restrictions with a smaller font or crowded layout. They'll know. They've known since college.

Then, save your work as a .doc or .pdf file. Some editors can't read any other kind of file. Name the file with the title of your piece for anonymous submissions, or with Title-Your Last Name for named submissions.

It's useful to have some of your pieces formatted and ready to go in .doc and .pdf files. That way, when you see an opportunity, sending your work is three simple steps—check the format against the guidelines, customize the cover letter, and send—instead of a big chore.

Cover Letters

Cover letters are always short. They always end with "Thank you for your time and consideration" or something similarly thankful, formal and neutral. About half the time, maybe more, no-one will bother to read it. But sometimes they will, so keep it short and professional.

If you've got a connection, mention it. If you don't, that's cool too. If you can find the editor's name (the one who handles your genre) use it, but many submissions are first read by graduate student assistants anyway.

Dear Editors:

I've enjoyed Gulf Stream for several months now—I'm a native Floridian and found you through Connie May Fowler's work, after hearing her speak at Eckerd College, my alma mater. The variety of essay forms that appear in your pages is inspiring—recently I especially loved Jonathan Callard's "New Country."

Below is my 1250-word nonfiction piece, "Nama," written from my experiences learning Japanese and cheating on my husband.

I'm an emerging writer; so far I've had essays in The New York Times and Travelers' Tales: Prague, and short stories in Crossed Genres and The Drum audio literary magazine. I'm also a two-time winner of The Moth StorySLAM.

Thank you for your time and consideration,

Allison K Williams

Dear Editors:

I've enjoyed Boulevard for a year now—Josip Novakovich's "Balkan Express" got me started, as it so perfectly captured many of my own experiences traveling in Eastern Europe.

Attached is my own 1700-word nonfiction piece, "Kalighat," written from a trip to India last year. I told a version of the story at The Moth StorySLAM in Chicago (and won), and thought it might also make a more formally-written essay.

I'm an emerging writer; so far I've had essays in The New York Times and Travelers' Tales: Prague, and short stories in Crossed Genres and The Drum audio literary magazine.

Thank you for your time and consideration,

Allison K Williams

Notice that it's the same basic information, tailored to the piece I'm submitting and the place it's going to. These are the longest a cover letter should ever be.

Those sound a little suck-up.

I agree. But people appreciate knowing that you liked something they did. These days, I mostly just write "Attached please find my essay Title" and do a short bio rather than an actual letter.

What if I don't have any publication credits?

Then your letter will be shorter. But put in something that lets them make a connection with you.

Dear Editors:

I've enjoyed reading One Story for several months now. It's always a delight to find it in the mailbox!

Submitted herewith is my 2400-word essay, "Knitted."

I'm a teacher living in Kalamazoo, Michigan, where I host a weekly knitting club and enjoy waterskiing.

Thank you for your time and consideration,

Priya Patel

If you're writing nonfiction and you have something that gives you credibility, put it in briefly (as above).

Do not ever under any circumstances describe your plot. Not even a brisk summary. Let the editor come to your piece as a fresh eye. If it doesn't work without an explanation—as a reader will come to it—it's not ready to send out.

A lot of journals accept work through Submittable (see Chapter Eight). There is a small box to put a personal statement/cover letter, and you can be short and casual there:

> Thanks for considering "Buddha Nature."

> My previous work has appeared in The Kenyon Review Online, Brevity, and the New York Times.

In the end, very few editors care about your resume—they care about your work.

Write down the elements that will become your cover letter:

- Your publication history. If you don't have one, you're an "emerging writer."

- Your biography as a writer. You could include writing groups you belong to, any degrees, prizes, etc. If you don't have any, one sentence about your life is perfect: "I live in Kalamazoo, Michigan, where I enjoy gardening and collect French cookware."

- Boil the above info down into four sentences. Write two versions: the "I am" version in first person and the "Allison is" version in third person. Some magazines ask for a cover letter; others specify a bio, for which you can use your third-person version.

Write your cover letter:

- Keep it short and professional.

- When you've picked a place to submit, look at their most recent issue (it's often online). If you can truthfully say something brief about a piece you liked, throw that in.

- If there's an editor's name on the masthead or website, use it! Otherwise, "Dear Editor" is fine.

- Do not summarize explain, describe, or set up the piece you're sending in. It must stand alone to the reader. If your piece needs explanation, it's not ready to go.

- Do not describe yourself as "unpublished," or say or imply that writing is your hobby. You might be an "early-career" writer, but it still counts.

Your cover letter won't always be read, or it's often read by the intern who screens the email. Write it anyway, for the editors who want it and read it.

Submittable

Submittable: so much better than stealing photocopies at our temp jobs or wondering if no response means "lost in the mail."

If you're not already using Submittable, the site is a service for authors to submit work to literary magazines, and for magazines a way to control and organize the tsunami of submissions without letting anyone slip through the cracks. In terms of paper saved, Submittable is probably responsible for half a rainforest.

Basically, you create a free account and can upload your work to magazines via their submission pages that direct you to their Submittable page. It saves typing in your name and address every time, and it keeps a list of everything you've submitted and its status as Received, In-Progress, Accepted, Completed, Declined, Withdrawn.

Not that we're checking it every day or anything...

Submittable's blessing and curse is the author seeing more of the submission process. You can see where your submission is in a journal's pipeline, and some editors handle edits through the site. It's also easy to "withdraw" a piece, but be warned— the editor gets an email letting them know, so it's not for "Oh I don't think they've read it yet and I just did a better draft."

Slideroom is a similar service geared more towards visual artists, but several writing residencies use it for applications, and you may come across a few journals using it.

7. Sending Out Submissions

It's time to be shoved out of the nest and start sending out your work. (It's going to be OK, I promise—it won't always be fun, but it will be OK.) Just as you methodically made your list of magazines, wrote your cover letter, and formatted your work, submitting has methods, too.

Take another look at your self-evaluation from Chapter Three, and your goals from Chapter Two. Pull up your spreadsheet from Chapter Five. Who is publishing work like yours, a little bit higher-level, or a little bit below your level? Make a Top Ten list of where you want your work to appear. It's a little like applying to college:

- Choose three journals that are a stretch—they're a little bit better than what you're writing right now.

51

- Choose three that are safer—you write a little bit better than they publish, but they pay, or you like the magazine, or this is a place for something strong but not your very best piece, or it's a niche market that you fit exactly.

- Choose four that are on the nose—you write at the level they publish, and they fit your goal for Publication, Prestige or Payment.

- For each one, read several pieces from their archives, in your genre. If you're a poet, read a bunch of poems. If you write fiction, read the short stories. Notice the magazine's overall style—traditional literary stories? Flash? Multimedia poems? Can you imagine your work in that company?

- Some places have submission fees. Take a look and see if you think it's worth it. Usually the fees are to weed out non-serious submitters (like students with an assignment to "submit something"), but sometimes they can be a money-maker for the magazine. Trust your own opinion.

- If you're writing something for a specific column or a regular feature (like a newspaper's weekly personal essay), read 15-20 previous pieces in the series, to see if you're in line with the style, structure, length and content. If you're shooting for Modern Love, look online for everything the editor has written about his selection process.

If you discover that any of your journal choices feel like a worse fit than you thought, replace it with another choice from your spreadsheet.

Then prepare your submissions.

- ✒ Check each magazine's website for editors' names, format, word count and any relevant deadlines. Not every magazine reads submissions year-round—some have "open reading" periods and times when they are closed to submissions.

- ✒ Look up any interviews with the editor online. They may have discussed what attracts them to particular work, or specific elements they look for.

- ✒ Format your submission. Many journals say on their website what they want your submission to look like—author's name on every page or only on the cover letter, page numbers, margins, etc. Explore your beautiful creativity in your material, not your layout. Almost everyone wants double-spaced (single-spaced for poetry), 12-point Times New Roman (or another common and easily read serif font), and one-inch margins.

- ✒ Briefly personalize your cover letter for each magazine and save it as a .doc or .pdf. You'll either be attaching files in the format they request, or copy-pasting into a form.

- ✒ Most magazines want to be the first one to print your work. Some of them classify material posted to your personal blog as "previously published." On a practical level, if you have a very small readership, you can mark those posts private when you're ready to submit. On an ethical level, do enough revisions that you can describe the blog post as "an earlier draft."

Prepare a "rejection ritual" that reminds you that each 'no' is proof you are sending your work into the world, and another step towards 'yes.' Make a list of your favorite authors' rejection numbers, or make sure you have a friend who will console you and help you move on. Remember that rejection often doesn't mean "not good enough"—it means "not right for us right now." There are lots of people-of-the-gender-you're-attracted-to who are "good enough," but you don't want to date all of them, right?

Send submissions to your Top Ten.

1) Pick a magazine from your list

2) Double-check everything one more time. Proper format? Named or blind? Within their word limits, genre specifications, addressed to the right editor, in a file format they ask for?

3) Then hit send on that email or upload that file to Submittable.

4) Log the submission in your spreadsheet so you know where you sent it, with a note saying how long the magazine takes to respond.

Pat yourself on the back for doing your writing work. Then forget it.

No seriously, let it vanish from your mind entirely. No

hoping, no wishing, no waiting, no wanting. Instead, start looking up the next magazine.

Oh man I really want to win that contest! I'm going to only eat with my left hand as a lucky talisman! = sadness and depression when you don't even place.

The reaction you want to have is, *Huh, I sent this to Journal X? Guess I must have. OK, tick them off the spreadsheet for a few months. Who else would love this piece? And what else can I send Journal X a couple months from now?* That's why you're sending ten at a time—it's harder to passionately care about ten submissions than it is about one.

Repeat this process as often as you like.

—·—

Some writers recommend submitting each piece ten different places. I prefer to pick likely places, or ones I really want, and send out ten different pieces at once. The only hard and fast rule (as we discussed in Chapter Five) is:

When your piece is accepted, you must IMMEDIATELY notify every other journal where you submitted that hasn't rejected it yet.

Not tomorrow. Not later tonight. RIGHT NOW. It's not rude to submit to more than one place–but it's rude to let them think they have a chance if they don't.

If you receive a rejection, note that in your spreadsheet, along with any feedback you received. You won't get any feedback at all most of the time—they don't have time. (Would you have time to explain to every person who looked at you on the street just why you don't want to date them?) If you get any feedback at all, that's a very good sign! Especially if you receive a personalized rejection that encourages you to submit other work: they really mean it, and you should send something else in about two months, or in their next reading period. It is actually a plus that most places take forever to respond. Instead of a stab, it's more a pang of disappointment, or even, Oh good, I wrote something better in the meantime and maybe they'll take that piece instead.

Finally, remember that submitting your work for publication is a process, not a product. Even famous writers still get rejections. The more pieces you send out to the more places, the less any one rejection stings. And the more you carefully investigate where to send your work, the more likely you are to be successful. For me, the very best part of the submission process is getting ideas for new things to write, based on what magazines say they're looking for. And that's always a win!

Simultaneous Submissions

On a trip to India, I discovered Madhubani, a type of painting made only in Bihar, a state in the north of India. At a government-run store, I saw quite a few I liked, but didn't have cash on me. The salesclerk graciously held them for two days, and I went back and bought them.

Now imagine I asked the clerk to hold the paintings for six months, while I looked at other paintings, left India, and later sent an email saying I didn't want them after all. Or thought, "they'll just assume I don't want them when they don't hear back."

That's what "no simultaneous submissions" is.

I understand—Literary magazines often have small staffs, squeezing in reading whenever they can while publishing a magazine or a website on no money as everyone's third job. However, that being their labor of love doesn't make it mine. "No simultaneous submissions" asks me, the writer, to leave my product—the only thing that generates income for me—in their editorial hands while they take the time they need to decide if they want it.

Gentle Editors, if you want an exclusive look at my work, get a reader on staff and read faster. Hire your teenage kid to weed out anything with more than three spelling errors on the first page. Get a college intern to pull the ten best submissions each day. Learn to write fast form rejections; learn to read the first page and know. Or accept simultaneous submissions.

Some writers worry they'll get a bad reputation if they withdraw a piece from a "no simultaneous submissions" venue. But if the journal responds slowly because they have thousands of submissions, they aren't going to remember who I am. If they're slow because they can't get it together, then do I really care?

A magazine that handles this well is The Sun. They "discourage simultaneous submissions" but do not forbid them. They are up front about their policy, pay well, and are a high-prestige venue. If I submit a piece to The Sun, it's because they are my first choice and worth the wait.

Unless a magazine specifically says "no simultaneous submissions," you can assume it's OK. Keep good records, and be quick to withdraw if your piece is accepted elsewhere

8. What Editors Think

Some days the submission process is a joyful flutter of anticipation--but let's face it, it's mostly a grind. And not just for the authors. Before I started regularly weeding through piles of incoming writing, I had a very specific image in my head:

> An overworked intern staggers through a door, arms piled high with envelopes. She chucks her armload at the base of an enormous pile of manuscripts, some half-out of their envelopes, others with footprints and pizza stains. Squatting atop the pile is Jabba the Hutt, wearing an old-fashioned editor's eyeshade and typing on a MacBook Air.

> Jabba speaks: "Well, Emily, another delivery of hopeless crap? Why do you add them to my Pile of Sadness? Why not just cast them directly into the Pit of Rejection, where they

will burn in wretchedness for eternity! BWA
HA HA HA HA."

Sometimes in my nightmare there's a dart board, on
which the choicest bits of literary failure are impaled,
a group of hipsters mocking each submission as they
keep score.

But now that I've seen the other side of the process,
nothing is farther from the truth. Most of the time,
most magazines read every single submission. Most
of the time, most editors open the email with a sense
of anticipation, wanting the writing to be not just
good but amazing, something they'll be proud to
publish, and thrilled the writer thought to send it to
their journal.

They want you to be good.

They want to hold your work to their breast and sigh,
"This is why I'm an editor. This poem/essay/story."
They don't want to read a thousand submissions, they
want the first sixty to be so amazing they can close
down submissions for the year.

They want to open the first batch of emails and say,
"Well, that's it, we've filled the next issue! Let's go get
gluten-free pizza."

And when a submission's not right for the
magazine—whether it's a near miss or a total
misfire—there is very little gleeful cackling. An editor
is more likely to sigh and say, "I wish I could talk to
them about what's working in this piece and deserves
more space," or, "I wish it was my place to tell them

to rewrite this in past tense, third person," or even "I wish I had time to make a list of magazines this piece would be perfect for." But there is so rarely enough time. The editor has fifty more essays to read that day, before grading the papers they really meant to do over the weekend except the dog was sick and the sitter cancelled.

Sometimes an editor makes time, and those are the best rejections to get. The ones that show somebody read this, somebody thinks it's close. The type of rejection that sends an author back to the typewriter instead of out to the bar. If you get a personalized rejection, or one that asks you to submit again, they really do mean it and you should. Don't revise and resubmit the same piece unless it's been specifically asked for, and give them breathing time. Send a new piece six to eight weeks later.

But when it's been a long month of form rejections, it's easy to get discouraged, to find yourself thinking:

It's all a rigged game. If you're not already famous, no-one wants you. It's impossible to get an agent or editor's attention. It's impossible to get pulled from the slush pile. It's impossible to know what they want.

This is incorrect.

Ten minutes on the internet and you can find out exactly what editors and agents are looking for. They write it on their websites. They publish work they like and you can read it and learn their tastes. There's a whole site, QueryShark, devoted to (helpfully) critiquing query letters for novels. There's at least one agent who gives personal responses instead of rejection letters a few times a year, which she announces in advance on her blog.

Yes, there are a thousand submissions in the inbox. Maybe more. But here's a secret:

The odds are in your favor.

The actual odds. (Collated from my friend the mid-size publisher, my friend the small publisher, my experience as an editor of an academic journal and a literary journal, and from interviews with agents.) You're not competing with every other submission.

If we randomly pull 100 submissions from any given slush pile:

50

are wrong. They have been sent to the wrong place— i.e., a short story to a poetry-only magazine, or a novel to a publisher that only prints playscripts. These lost souls are a waste of time and postage that five minutes looking up submission guidelines would have saved.

40

are terrible. They are poorly spelled, un-grammatical, the story is leaden and boring, the characters hack-neyed, the plot a thin copy of the latest trend. The authors should stick their work in a drawer, write a lot more, raise their level, and come back in five years to see if anything is salvageable about this one.

are good but not good enough. The author needs another draft, maybe two. They're on the down side of a trend instead of the up side. The journal just published something on this theme last month. The piece isn't bad, but it doesn't click for the editor who reads it. You'll know you fit in this category when your rejection has a few personal lines, or a suggestion about what to fix. Take it seriously—even one personal sentence is gold. My co-editor at the academic journal was mystified at how many authors didn't understand that a four-page revise-and-resubmit letter wasn't a rejection, it was "We want your next draft." No-one spends more time than they have to on a real rejection.

And that 100th manuscript? It's good. And while there's still the chance that it's not quite in line with this editor's taste, it's only one in a hundred.

If you have truly, truly, put the time and effort in to make your work as good as it can be—which takes months or years, plus feedback from trusted friends and critiques from people you aren't sleeping with or near, and possibly even editing you've paid for, plus reading everything you can in your genre or field to know what trends are coming and what are played out, and reading everything you can from and about the venues you want to sell to—you are not competing with the whole slush pile.

You are competing with one in a hundred.

Your dream publication has a thousand manuscripts?

You only have to be better than nine.

And that's pretty good odds.

Calibrating: Clues From The Submission Process

Ideally, your work will go in waves.

First, submit to places where you are "just right" or shooting a little high. If after 10-20 submissions you get only form rejections back (or nothing), either the piece isn't ready or you're aiming too high. Adjust the level of magazine you're sending your work to, and keep examining and improving your writing.

When you start getting rejections back with a personal note, or an invitation to send something else, you are playing in the right ballpark.

If you get a response with suggested revisions and a request to send it back in with changes, that is a terrific positive sign. Many writers take this as "They think my work is terrible and want to change it!" Nope. They think your work is lovely and want to make a place for it in their publication. Help them do this. Examine their feedback carefully, maybe bounce it off a writer buddy. Make the changes you agree will improve the piece. If they suggest a change you feel is wrong, see if you agree there's a problem that needs to be addressed, and solve it a different way.

Eventually, you'll see your rate of acceptances increase. Now start looking for magazines that are at a similar level. This, and reaching a little higher, is your ballpark right now.

9. Rejection Is Good. Really.

As a writer, there is only one way to avoid rejection: don't submit your work. As successful and rejection-free as Emily Dickinson's career was, most of us would like to achieve the bulk of our publication prior to death.

Rejection sucks. It sucks every time, whether it's a big suck or a little suck. But it's part of the process. It's part of being a writer. It's a badge that says "I'm serious about this and I'm sending out my work." Think about, say, gymnasts, and how many times they hit the mat hard, face-first, before getting a new skill. Or car salesmen, and how many customers they talk to before a single closing. Or chefs, who offer a whole menu, but you only eat one thing. Writing is not the only job full of "trying."

From the editors' perspective, think about how many times you've walked into a car dealership and turned down a salesman—you didn't hate him, but he didn't have what you were looking for. You needed a blue minivan and all he had was a red convertible. It doesn't make the convertible a lousy car—but it's not what you needed that day. Think about how many dishes you've looked at on menus and not ordered. That's what reading the submission pile is like. *I had that yesterday…Love that, but I always order it…I'm not hungry enough for pasta…* If we see pistachio ice cream and pick chocolate instead, the chef in the back is not moaning, "My pistachio must be terrible." Nor is he coming out with a cleaver, shouting "How dare you not like pistachio!" He accepts that different diners have different tastes.

What we can do as writers to deal with rejection is twofold:

1) Accept that it's part of the job.

It's not a personal hate, it's not mean, it's not the establishment failing to appreciate your talent. You just didn't have the piece they needed today. Tomorrow that might change. Either you'll find a home for the piece somewhere else, or you'll find another piece for this publication, or you'll write another piece. Or all of the above.

2) Actively make it part of the job.

Every third month, I like to do a submissions blitz (SUBMIT ALL THE THINGS!). I commit to sending out a piece every single day for a month. Some days I send in something I already have in a file, some days I come across a submissions call and write something specifically for it. I dash off or copy-paste a cover letter, make sure my essay or story or pitch is formatted according to their requests, hit send, and log it in my chart. If I miss a day, I send out two the next day.

What this process does for me is reduce the sting of any single rejection. The first one usually hurts for about a day. The second one hurts for a couple of hours. But by the time the fifteenth rejection trickles in six months later, I'm not going "Ouch!" anymore. I'm saying, "Wait, who are you? What did I send you? Oh, cross that off." By the time I hit thirty submissions, usually at least one has been accepted (which gives me the pleasure of withdrawing it from other places).

The more regularly you submit—and if you can't do a blitz, try for something reasonable like once a week—the less any given rejection will bother you. It becomes routine. You become the nine-year-old gymnast slamming into the mat and getting up to try it again. You become the chef thinking, *nobody's ordered pistachio in a while, maybe I should take it off the menu and do some rum raisin.*

All in a day's work.

Resubmitting

Once or twice a year, I declare a month "Submit All the Things!" and send out a piece to a journal, literary website, or a radio show every day. Thirty or thirty-one submissions (choosing February seems like cheating), formatted and cover-lettered and sent, click, click, click. I'm all about the scattershot approach—rejections drift in slowly over the next six months or so, and by the time my next submission blitz rolls around, I don't even remember what got turned down where (God bless spreadsheets!).

But what about the persistent, single-minded writer? *Missouri Review* editor Michael Nye once mentioned to a new intern that they'd received thirty stories over fifteen years from a single author. The intern asked, "How does someone keep sending work to a magazine that keeps rejecting the work?"

Getting rejected many times before landing a publication slot in a particular journal is common. Especially if the journal sends encouraging rejections, or "we'd like to see something else from you."

It takes more than ordinary persistence to keep sending out work in the face of form rejections and silence. It's hard for a writer to know if they're just missing the mark, or not playing in the same league.

How can you tell? How do you figure out where to submit your (different) work more than once?

By reading widely, working to improve your craft, and honestly assessing your own writing skill relative to where you want to publish.

It's important to keep raising your level, and look back at past work to see your growth. It's important to read widely within your genre so that you know where you really want to be published and what their standards are. It's important to stay humble and willing to accept feedback from trusted sources.

Be diligent with your work.

Be selective in your submissions.

Keep trying.

10. Literary Citizenship

Many new writers worry that the literary world is closed... a hotbed of nepotism, mutual back-scratching, and willful avoidance of anything or anyone from over the transom. And in a way it is–no matter what our level, whether our work is in the local coffee-house's literary journal or a respected national publication, writers read our friends, we read the people our friends told us to read, we read people with whom we have something in common, and then–if there's time–we read everyone else.

This can be deeply frustrating when a writer is starting out. At Literary Hub, writer/teacher/Instagrammer Jeff Sharlet wrote an open letter[4] to a stranger convinced his work is being overlooked, about how Sharlet sets priorities for his limited reading time:

---

4 "When a Self-Described Genius Asks You To Read His Masterpiece" http://lithub.com/when-a-self-declared-genius-asks-you-to-read-his-masterpiece/

You seem indignant that I've not read your work; you don't mention whether or not you've read mine; and you can't imagine that there might be work by those besides you—besides me!—worth reading.

For instance, work by young writers, students, for whom I'm often the only reader. You could say, "Sure, but those kids are privileged, they can afford college." Fair enough. But reading their work is the job that allows me to afford groceries. It has the added benefit of being deeply pleasurable, in part because so few students presume their own genius. They tend to be grateful for a single reader, even one who's slow, sometimes, because he procrastinates by answering crank emails from strangers.

Another category of writer worth reading: Friends. "Oh, great," you might say, "a chummy clique of established writers." That's true. But then, there's the fact that we weren't always "established," and the reality that for all but the most famous or most self-satisfied writers, being "established"—published and sometimes paid—doesn't mean you don't depend on friends to ping back like sonar when you drop some new work into the abyss of public words.

Sharlet discusses the circumstances that create communities of mutual readers, and how literary citizenship arises inextricably from personal connection–but also, how that "personal" connection isn't something that springs into being fully formed. Personal connections and literary "friends" are cultivated and maintained, largely through mutual interest in each other's words and subject matter.

Are you reading your friends' work? Are you reading the places you want to be published, and having small interactions in person or in email or on social media? Are you looking for places to meet other writers online or in person, in workshops, classes, forums and interest groups? Are you reading widely in the subjects or genres you care about most, and letting those authors know you exist and you appreciate their work? Those are the first steps. And what we're all heading for is not tumbling down the walls of the literary Jericho we stand outside in supplication, but creating a new world of our own. One holding the citizens we most admire, encompassing the writers who came up with us and ourselves.

Some actions you can take as a literary citizen:

EASY: Set up a Twitter account, and follow literary magazines and writers whose work you like. If you're already active on Twitter, set up a List of these accounts so you have them all in one place, rather than having to hunt through your whole feed. Once a week (or while you're waiting in the carpool line or for the dentist or for your food to arrive already), retweet things you like. Read at least one linked piece, and if you like it, tweet about it, mentioning the author's name and/or the publication. If you prefer Facebook, post a weekly link to something you enjoyed reading, with a compliment and/or a choice quote. Both Twitter and Facebook reposts help writers and journals; with Twitter they are more likely to know you're there. If you keep a blog, post a short excerpt, your thoughts, and a link to the whole piece. (Never repost a whole piece without permission and hopefully payment.)

MEDIUM: Go to your local bookstore and purchase a couple of literary magazines. Enjoy reading them. Don't feel obligated to read cover-to-cover—that's how we end up with a stack of New Yorkers in the bathroom. If there's a piece you really like, find out if it's online and tweet about it or post it to your Facebook. If you are resolutely anti-social-media, write a quick note and mail it—fan mail is one of the most incredible and encouraging things a writer can receive.

MEDIUM: Find a Facebook or other online group for writers who share your genre or interests. Read the other writers' work and participate in discussions. A good group can be a place to find publication opportunities, upcoming workshops (online and real-life), new books you'd like to read, commiseration about writing problems and discussions on how to solve them.

CHALLENGING: Bond with one or more fellow writers by asking if anyone wants to swap work and read for each other. Give excellent feedback, which is not the same thing as expert feedback. Don't worry about your literary "credentials" or your educational background. It's OK to slowly learn to give better feedback. Start by saluting the author, say what you received from the piece (literal plot and emotional impact), point out three specific things you liked, and three things they might keep working on or questions you had. For example:

> *Thanks for asking me to read! What I got was that this is a nonfiction essay about the time you went boating with your dad, with a larger theme of re-negotiating the parent-child relationship. It felt reflective and lyrical.*

> *I really loved the image of the oarlocks, I could really see your dad's hands, and that made the power imbalance in the relationship clear. The lake felt like an intimidating and ominous place. And the way you detoured into the dream at the end was really effective—I thought it conveyed the transient nature of parent-child bonding moments.*

I found myself wanting to know more about the boathouse—it seemed like the implication was something bad had happened there, but I didn't know what. In the fifth paragraph, the autumn leaves are a great picture but feel superfluous, like other sections of the story (the shoreline, taking down the oars) are already covering that ground. And I know it's picky-picky, but when you're at that stage, you might double-check the punctuation in the dialogue (commas go inside quotes).[5]

Notice that the overall tone is respectful, self-effacing, and grateful to have been entrusted with someone's precious work. Note also that non-specific praise and criticism are not useful, and one of the greatest compliments you can pay another writer is to believe they are ready, willing and able to accept constructive feedback.

4) EXTRA CREDIT: Get involved in person in a literary community of some kind. Volunteer for a literary magazine that needs help addressing envelopes or updating their mailing list. Go to a workshop taught by a local writer. Attend a writing conference, and keep up with the people you met there via social media.

---

5. We are assuming this writer is using American punctuation.

Are You a Writer?

Everyone struggles with feeling fraudulent, or like they "aren't there yet." A few years ago, when I was changing jobs from entertainer to writer, I ended up as a plus-one at a fancy music-industry party at the Savoy Hotel in London. The ballroom was very blue and white and gilt, and full of mostly older music industry types, the kind of people whose program bios featured casual snapshots of themselves with various Beatles. Over the luncheon, risotto with fennel (yum!) and quince sauerkraut (just as not-good as it sounds), someone asked, "Oh you're from the States, what do you do?"

Um…

I used to say "trapeze artist" because I was, and that was easy (you're already starting that conversation in your head, right?). Now, I've published essays and won prizes, had my byline in places I admire. But compared to my friend and his book deal and my other friend and his three-book deal, I feel like one of the stepsisters trying to get her size 11W into the shoe. I haven't sold any books, how can I possibly say I'm a writer?

Farther back on the publishing trajectory we may not feel like "real" writers. Finishing a piece and publishing a piece and getting an agent and getting a book deal are the successive badges that say *I did it* or *I am it* and each of those things punches our ticket; validation. Claiming the title before the accomplishments can feel like misrepresentation.

But at the same time, I remember how, before circus, I first became a theatre director:

By telling people I was one.

I worked community theatre gigs and high school gigs, and eventually college guest artist spots and professional positions. Every time I met someone in theatre I'd say, "I'm a director," and when they asked what I'd done lately I described one of my shows without being specific about the level I was working at. "Oh yeah, we put Puck in a mask and the whole stage was a giant bed…" (I didn't mention they were high-school sophomores).

It's not a lie. It's not a fraud. It's not getting above ourselves.

It's starting a conversation.

Sure, you may not be a published writer. You may not be a full-time writer. You may be an early-career writer. But you know what? Published writers don't get everything they write published. People who make a living writing almost always teach or edit or freelance on the side.

You are what you present yourself as. You have a right to define yourself, and project that definition to others. Every time you say what you want to be is what you are, you help move yourself ahead and you let others help you move ahead. Like dressing for the job you want to be hired for.

Imagine you're chatting with, say, Cheryl Strayed and

the guy who owns your local indie bookstore. When they ask if you're a writer, and you say, "Oh, no, not yet," the conversation ends there. But when you say (modestly), "I'm working on a memoir about my time in the military," or "I'm excited about sending around my new travel essay series," that opens a door for them to help you. Yes, they might say "Oh, nice," and smile blankly. But they might respond with, "I'd love to see a few pages when you're done," or "Make sure you query so-and-so, I hear they're looking for that," or "Do you know about our reading series for local authors?" All of those responses create dialogue. They help you bond with the larger community. They make connections. Even if you're not ready for a particular opportunity yet, you're becoming more familiar with your literary community.

Being a "writer" is like being a "dancer" or a "parent." You are a dancer when you dance—you are a parent the entire life of your child. Because our work exists in a recorded and fixed form, we tend to use production of fixed forms—books—as benchmarks of our success. But being a writer is a process. When you show up at the page, it is like showing up at the barre. It is like listening to your child when you're not sure you're about to make the right decision. Writing is a process rather than a destination.

There is no certification for writers, no governing body, no guild. We have permission to define ourselves, and we should define ourselves as worthy. Presenting ourselves as part of the group helps others see us as worth their time and energy. Worth, eventually, their dollars and their reading.

When I got home that gathering from London, I ordered new business cards.

They said *Writer.*

Making A Writing Life

Part of what helps us feel like "real" writers is having the actions of writing as part of our daily life. In Chapter Three, we talked about evaluating your own writing level and working to improve your craft by analyzing other writers' work. As a literary citizen, you're also getting involved as a reader, informal publicist, fan and critique partner. How does all this fit into your routine?

Write with a plan. Decide what you want to improve about your work. Challenge yourself. Write when it's not easy, when you're not inspired, when you have nothing to say. Write when it isn't fun, when it's a slog up the mountain in the rain. Easy accomplishment is cheap; fighting for the words and winning—even barely, even when it's not your best work—lets you know you can do it again.

Vary your style. Write work that stands alone. Write serial chapters so strong people want to read what they're from. Write genres you're not interested in— you may surprise yourself. Write short pieces to show the power of your brevity. Write long pieces to show your staying power. Remember that short attention spans can be your friend; standing among 300 can make you shout louder or whisper more piercingly.

Connect with new writers in the real world and online, even if the interaction is short. Choose friends outside the literary world to share your work with. Get feedback from writers and co-workers and readers of every level from "read a beer bottle once" to "better writer than you ever dare hope to be."

Be supportive. But when you think someone is ready for it, when you're brave enough, when you've built a relationship of encouragement and support, give the best critique you can. Give honest feedback. Make your motivations clear. Stay direct even when polite. Tell it like you see it, but tactfully.

Be generous. With your time, with your talent, with your encouragement and feedback. Read everything you can—strategically, you'll know what you're up against; competitively, you'll be challenged and inspired. Comment on everything. We all feel like we're howling into the void, and even "Enjoyed reading!" is a lifeline from the dock of humanity we're paddling so desperately toward. Being "popular" and being engaged in the community are the same behavior with different hats.

Be ambitious. Be brave. Be ruthless. Be raw. Write about pomegranates and roller coasters and cement mixers. Write about your relationship and your relationship with your mother and your relationship with your depression. Write to honor your dead. If you are going to write about the zombie apocalypse you had better have something damn original to say.

Put writing first. Stay up late. Get up early. Make it the top of the list, above laundry and getting paid and sometimes above lunch. Skip out on your other responsibilities. If you're an overachiever, narrow your focus. Trust that your children will learn to feed themselves, your boyfriend will manage his socks, shaved legs are overrated. And if you can't put writing first, that's OK, too—put it where you can.

This book is about getting published, but publication is not what makes you a writer. That's not what makes any of us writers—artists—winners. You write, you write, always you write, and in the end, you win because you show up.

Show up to the page. Show up to the community. Show up to your colleagues' writing. Show up to the new writers and the bad writers and the teenage writers and the writers you know who aren't even planning on showing their work to anyone but still need to know they're not alone. Show up with your voice. Show up with your style. Show up with what you love and why it matters, and lay it on the page, naked and alone and afraid, but showing up.

It will be terrifying.

You may feel like you are howling into the void. You are, but there are others in the void, howling back.

And as long as you keep howling, you win.

You win.

You win by being there, and you win by being able to write about it, and by writing about it even when you're not able, when you are crippled and limping and the pen in your hand is running low on ink and all your paper is wet with tears.

You win.

And the cruelest joke the universe plays is that when you win, it's not the end of the game. It's getting bumped up to a higher level with harder obstacles, and you can never go back and be satisfied playing the level you already beat.

I have one more secret. That when you show up, and you reach out with generosity, and you do your best work or your second-best work and summon up the bravery to share it, you create a community. You, a writer, the loneliest of artists, become part of a team. And even when you are home alone, sweating in the Louisiana heat and cursing things that buzz, or walking down 5th and wondering if there might be just one affordable place in this city of strangers and darkness while gearing up to freeze your ass off for the next four months, you are still playing as part of a team. They are in the shadows and they are on the other end of the internet and they are reading your words and saying,

me, too.

Me, too.

11. Your Reading List

Your reading list is not just where you want to publish, but also where you get ideas. It's where you find out what's going on in the world, what you care about enough to write, and where your voice fits in the larger literary world. Yes, craft is still the hard part, but the stimulation of new ideas helps sustain the excitement of creation.

As a working writer, you'll want to have a list of places you regularly read. Remember that tiny bits are OK—read a single poem on the subway, or a flash essay while you're waiting in the carpool line. Don't saddle yourself with "must read this journal cover-to-cover," let it be organic. Read what catches your eye.

You might start with a monthly plan of:

- Three places you'd like to be published, which could be websites, newspapers, commercial or literary magazines, etc.

- Three authors who blog about their writing process
- Regular visits to a writers' forum like She Writes or Absolute Write
- One piece of criticism or a review.
- One journal you've never read (a new one each time)

Here's what I read at least a little of every month.

Places I want to be published:

- *Harper's* (print)
- The *Atlantic* (print, but I'm stopping when my sub-scription runs out, and now I only skim it—not my market)
- The *New York Times* (online, articles here and there online, every Modern Love, every Lives, and the Travel section)
- The *New Yorker* (print, everything but most of the fiction)
- *McSweeney's Internet Tendency*
- *Lucky Peach* (print, back issues)
- A travel magazine (print, picked up at the airport, airport, usually *Afar* or *Condé Nast Traveler*)
- *The Rumpus* (online)
- *Slate* (online)
- The magazine on any flight I take, not thoroughly, but to see what they're publishing

- The alternative paper in any town I visit that has one (many of them run a yearly fiction contest)

Websites that keep me up to date on the market:

- *The Review Review*
- *Brevity*'s nonfiction blog[6]
- *Essay Daily*
- Who Pays Writers?
- A couple of Facebook groups for writers—I'm in groups for travel writers, memoirists, essayists, free-lancers and editors

Blogs by authors, agents, and sites that inspire me with their writing style or give me ideas:

- By Ken Levine (TV and movie writing)
- Penelope Trunk (philosophy of work)
- The Bloggess (personal blog that hit big, her specialty is black comedy about depression)
- The Oatmeal (cartoons)
- Janet Reid (agent)
- The Rejectionist (author and lit mag publisher, feminist and culturally conscious reading)

What I listen to (shows I want to pitch stories to, or whose sound techniques I'm learning about for my own podcasting):

- How Sound (PRX)

6. Disclosure: I'm Brevity's social media editor

- 99% Invisible (Radiotopia)

- Reply All (Gimlet Media)

- This American Life (Chicago Public Media)

- Radiolab (WNYC)

- Love Me (CBC)

- Snap Judgment (WNYC)

- The Moth (independent)

Books I found useful:

- *Making a Literary Life* by Carolyn See

- *Bird By Bird* by Anne Lamott

- *The Forest for the Trees* by Betsy Lerner

- *Thunder and Lightning* by Natalie Goldberg

- *On Writing* by Stephen King

- *Steering the Craft* by Ursula K. LeGuin

- John McPhee's articles on writing in *The New Yorker*

- *The Mindful Writer* by Dinty W. Moore

- *The Art of Memoir* by Mary Karr

Written down all in one place, it looks overwhelming. But it's not about reading or listening for six hours a day. Usually, I wake up and put on a podcast while I get ready. More podcast in the car. Part of a magazine over lunch. A blog post on my phone while someone else drives. Two essays in journals at the coffee shop. If I'm submitting somewhere particular that week,

I'll read anywhere from three to ten pieces in a row. Literary magazines otherwise I mostly scan, and read one or two things thoroughly. A column or particular style of piece like Modern Love, I read thirty or forty of them, and do some basic structural analysis, perhaps make notes about how I would tell a story in their style.

You know what you like to read, where you're excited to see a new story. Start reading consciously, as part of your literary life.

12. Disinformation

Some closing thoughts.

What nobody tells you as an artist is that every project starts at the beginning. Not just the blank page, the empty stage, but that you have to re-establish your credentials and your quality every time. You can coast on reputation a little, but it doesn't last long if you don't deliver.

What nobody tells you is that praise—a standing ovation, a good review, your teacher's approval—makes you feel good for a day, but one line of internet criticism from a stranger reverberates in your skull forever.

"Frankly, I don't see what all the fuss is about."

(I tried to feel bad when that critic killed himself the next year, but I didn't.)

What nobody tells your husband is that writing 3000 words in a calm, soothing, supportive environment still leaves you too tired to call home at the end of the day. So does doing three twenty-minute shows.

And then feeling guilty about it. But not guilty enough to call.

What nobody tells you, the artist, the writer, is that spending an entire day being paid to do something you love is not the same as fun. It's often better than fun, but it's not fun. What nobody tells you is that spending an entire day being paid to do something you love is sometimes a lot less fun than spending an entire day doing something you love for free.

What nobody tells you is that selling out is strangely comforting. That once you've decided to package your product and suck a little corporate dick for the chance to show most of what you like to do but structured as a James Bond theme and wearing black and yellow because it goes with the logo, the large check that ensues will feel earned. That paying rent with your art money feels like finally growing up. That you probably can come up with five hundred words about margarine and even feel proud of making it sound like something people would eat. (Please don't.)

What nobody tells you is that if you believe in yourself and dream big dreams you will still come in second to someone who worked hard. Or to a talentless hack related to the producer. Or to someone sleeping with the editor. Or to your best friend whom you will have to congratulate as sincerely as possible. Or to someone no better than you and there will be no reason at all.

What nobody tells you is that if you believe in yourself and dream big dreams and work hard you can accomplish anything, but if you're willing to wear a sexy outfit while accomplishing it, or include vampires, you'll get paid a lot more.

What nobody tells you is that you have to be the kind of person who can hear a hundred no's before you get to yes, and that if you are not that kind of person, selling your art may not be for you. Here, let's practice:

No. No. No. No. No. No. No. No. No. No. No. I'll call you back. No. No. No. No. No. We went with someone else. No. No. No. No. No. No. No. No. No. No. My cousin will do it for free. No. No. No. No. No. No. No. No. This did not fit our needs at this time; we sincerely wish you the best of luck placing it elsewhere. No. No. No. No. No. NO. No. No. No. NO. No. No. No. No. No. No. No. No. No. No. No. No. No. No. No. No. No. No. No. No. No. No response means no. No. No. No. No. No. No. No. No. No. No. No. No. NO. Next! No. No. No. No. No. My boss said no. My editor said no. No. No. No. No. No. NO. Sorry. No. No.

No.

Speaking editorially, we should get to 'yes' here, but it's better to experience the dissatisfaction of having our expectations unfulfilled, so we can quit before dissatisfaction crushes us. Or, so we can immunize ourselves.

So we can say, I am blue. My work is blue. The blue of a thousand cerulean seas. The blue of Texas bluebells. The stunning blue of the sky from the top of the mountain. The deep blue of sapphires. The gentle blue of my mother's eyes. The best blue.

They might want red.

And what nobody tells you is that it's not up to you to be red, and that whether or not you want to make your blue more of a purple, or draw a crimson border around it, or pass out violet-tinted glasses to all your readers, it is a choice. Your choice. Your choice to change or stay the course, and neither of those are wrong.

It is not a cruel world full of no.

It is a beautiful world in which the one (or many) persons to whom your work—your particular, personal work—speaks are waiting for you. Waiting for you to grow, to revise, to polish, to publicize, to sell, to share. Waiting for you to make art they love and will pay for.

Go and find them.

Resources

The Review Review is my number-one recommendation. They review individual literary journals, interview editors about what they're looking for, give submission tips, and present great lists of journals looking for particular topics.
http://www.thereviewreview.net

Especially check out their advice on getting started with submissions.
http://thereviewreview.net/publishing-tips/yes-your-submission-phobia-holding-you-back

Poets and Writers is a print magazine with a solid website. Submissions calls, grants, residencies and publication opportunities are in the back of the magazine and in their Classifieds section on the website.
http://www.pw.org/classifieds

New Pages is a site for "news, information, and guides to literary magazines, independent publishers, creative writing programs, alternative periodicals, indie

bookstores, writing contests, and more."
http://www.newpages.com

Duotrope is a subscription-based service with a database of markets for literary work, calendars of deadlines, and information about publishing in magazines and journals.
https://duotrope.com/

Submission calls are listed at Mslexia.
https://mslexia.co.uk/submissions/

Submission calls and contests in your inbox! The CRWROPPS-B group on Yahoo posts about 20 opportunities a week.
http://groups.yahoo.com/neo/groups/CRWROPPS-B/info

Here's a sample of what their digest looks like:

CRWROPPS-B Digest Sample

```
1 Call for Submissions: Compose
Journal by aejos

2 call for submissions: VLP by aejos

3 special issue feature contest:
Crab Orchard Review by aejos

4 cw position: Dixie  State (UT) by
aejos

5 poetry book contest: Waywiser
```

Press by aejos

6 call for submissions: Bird's
Thumb by aejos

7a fiction contest: Tennessee Williams Festival by aejos

Messages

1 Call for Submissions: Compose
Journal

Tue Nov 5, 2013 8:43 am (PST) .
Posted by: aejos

Compose: A Journal of Simply Good
Writing is now accepting fiction,
poetry, nonfiction and artwork for
their Spring 2014 issue.

You can read their Fall 2013 issue
at http://composejournal.com/issues/
fall-2013/

Submission guidelines: http://com-
posejournal.com/submissions/

Contributors have included William
Logan, Ada Limon, Randall Mann,
Rebecca Hazelton, Rebecca Rosenblum,
Katrina Kenison, Amorak Huey, Hannah
Stephenson, and Marion Roach Smith.

2 call for submissions: VLP

Tue Nov 5, 2013 8:44 am (PST) .
Posted by: aejos

The Vermillion Literary Project
(VLP) at the University of South
Dakota is currently seeking submissions of poetry, short fiction, and
creative nonfiction for its April
2014 issue of the VLP magazine, the
University's only student-produced
literary journal. For submission
guidelines, visit http://sites.usd.
edu/projlit/vlp-magazine/submit-
your-work

This year's submission reading deadline is December 15.

I've only copied the first two here, but all seven
opportunities listed in the initial contents would be
there. Subscribe to CRWROPPS-B at
http://groups.yahoo.com/neo/groups/CRWROPPS-B/
info

Sample Contributor's Guidelines

Check out *The Christian Science Monitor*'s guidelines
in particular–very helpful, and includes samples of
what they've published before. (The *Monitor* publishes
emerging writers and pays.) Also below are links to
the guidelines for *Oxford American* (pays, high prestige, hard to get into) and *Subtropics* (midlevel, no
pay).

http://www.csmonitor.com/About/Contributor-guide-lines

http://www.oxfordamerican.org/pages/submission-guidelines/

http://www.english.ufl.edu/subtropics/submit.html

Lists of Literary Magazines

http://www.everywritersresource.com/topliterarymag-azines.html

http://www.perpetualfolly.com (under Blog, choose Literary Magazine Ranking)

http://thejohnfox.com/ranking-of-literary-journals/

http://www.newpages.com/magazines/literary-maga-zines (very comprehensive)

http://www.perpetualfolly.com (under Blog, choose Literary Magazine Ranking)

http://thejohnfox.com/ranking-of-literary-journals/

http://blogs.chi.ac.uk/shortstoryforum/literary-maga-zines-and-other-markets/

Paying Markets

Most commercial/popular magazines and newspapers pay. If a place is selling advertising on more than a page or two, they should also be paying writers. If they aren't, be wary.

Duotrope is a paid service (there's a free trial) that lists paying writing opportunities and has an online submission organizer. https://duotrope.com/

The Review Review's list of paying literary magazines.

http://www.thereviewreview.net/publishing-tips/show-me-literary-magazines-pay

http://writersweekly.com/this_weeks_article/000647_09242003.html (personal essays)

MediaBistro is a site for commercial media and mass-market magazines. They provide courses, resources for freelancers, and great interviews with editors on how to pitch articles and essays to particular magazines.
http://www.mediabistro.com

http://meghanward.com/blog/2011/09/21/20-places-to-publish-personal-essays/ (personal essays, mostly paying)

'Who Pays Writers' Sample Posts

Who Pays Writers is an invaluable resource that lists writer-supplied reports of getting paid (or not). Here's a sample of what their site looks like:

Washington City Paper

by Who Pays Writers? on November 4, 2013, 0 comments

Report: $100 for a 2-4,000 word fiction piece in print and online in 2013. Submission/spec (piece was written prior and then submitted for publication). Rights: The publication bought exclusive rights to publish the material first, then rights ultimately revert to me [notwithstanding the publication's ability to keep the material available as part of its digital archive or website, nonexclusively]

Continue reading

Pet Business Magazine

by Who Pays Writers? on November 3, 2013, 0 comments

Report: $300 for a 1200-word column in print, in 2013. Medium reporting. Ongoing/pre-existing relationship with editor or publication. Contract: Verbal or "handshake" agreement. "Rate is typical for other sections of this magazine as well."

Continue reading

Noisey

by Who Pays Writers? on November 2, 2013, 0 comments

Report: $50 for a 500-1000 word op-ed online in 2013. Cold pitch (no pre-existing relationship). "Payment can take a while, the editors do know this fact."

Continue reading

LA Weekly

by Who Pays Writers? on November 1, 2013, 0 comments

Report: $75 for a 500-1000 word Q&A/interviewin "West Coast Sound,"LA Weekly's music blog (online only). Medium reporting. Cold pitch (no pre-existing relationship). Previous reports for this publication: http://scratchmag.net/tag/la-weekly/

Editor Manjula Martin plans to maintain the site "as a free web resource as long as there's demand for it."
http://www.whopayswriters.com

Writing Communities

Meetup is a place to find writing groups local to your area.
http://www.meetup.com/

Wattpad is a site where writers post their work for feedback and reading. Remember, if you put it online, it's "published," which means not being able to submit your piece elsewhere.
http://www.wattpad.com

Sixfold is a writing contest where participants give each other feedback.
http://www.sixfold.org

Absolute Write is an online community aimed at supporting, encouraging and educating writers.
http://absolutewrite.com/

She Writes is another online community for support, information and connections, aimed at women writers.
http://www.shewrites.com/

On Writing and Privilege

"Peculiar Benefits" by Roxane Gay at *The Rumpus*
http://therumpus.net/2012/05/peculiar-benefits/

"The Year in Work" by Andrea Bennet at *Hazlitt*
http://hazlitt.net/feature/year-work

"How the Literary Class System is Impoverishing Literature" by Lorraine Berry at *LitHub*
http://lithub.com/the-literary-class-system-is-impoverishing-literature/

"Where's Literature's Class Diversity?" by Phoebe Maltz Bovy at *New Republic*
https://newrepublic.com/article/127063/wheres-literatures-class-diversity

Also Useful

Query Shark is more aimed at novelists, but the storytelling lessons are priceless.
http://www.queryshark.blogspot.com

Preditors and Editors covers scams, bogus agents, and scurrilous publishing practices.
http://pred-ed.com/

Writer Beware! also deals with publishing scams and bad contests.
http://accrispin.blogspot.com

Janet Reid's agent blog covers a lot of standard literary practice. More for novelists, but it's a good place

to learn about literary citizenship.
http://jetreidliterary.blogspot.com/

About the Author

Guerrilla memoirist, essay writer, playwright and travel journalist, Allison Williams has written about race, culture and comedy for National Public Radio, the Canadian Broadcasting Corporation, the *New York Times*, *The Christian Science Monitor*, *McSweeney's Internet Tendency*, *Prairie Schooner*, *Kenyon Review Online* and *Travelers' Tales*. She currently serves as Social Media Editor for *Brevity*.

Her fiction has appeared in *Crossed Genres, Smokelong Quarterly, Deep South* and *The Drum*; her plays include the Heidemann Award finalist *Miss Kentucky,* scripts for NPR's All Ears Theatre, and the London Fringe Best Of Fringe winner, *TRUE STORY*.

She received her MFA from Western Michigan University and has been a teaching fellow at the Prague Summer Program and the Kenyon Writers Workshop (with Dinty W. Moore), and an Associate Artist at the Atlantic Center for the Arts with Rick Moody, Dani

Shapiro and David Shields.

As a storyteller, Allison has performed at London's Theatre Royal and Rich Mix, Filocafe in Mumbai and The Kautilya Society in Varanasi, India, and is a two-time winner of The Moth StorySLAM. As an aerialist and acrobat, she performed in 23 countries.

Home base is currently Dubai, where "The Pork Shop" is a separate, dimly-lit room at the back of the super-market. It's like buying meat porn.

Find her at www.idowords.net.

Made in United States
North Haven, CT
17 January 2022

14813085R00069